THE TIME I DIDN'T KNOW WHAT TO DO NEXT

The Time I Didn't Know What to Do Next

J. Stephen Rhodes

Introduction by Leatha Kendrick

For Connie

WIND PUBLICATIONS

The Time I Didn't Know What to Do Next.
Copyright © 2008 by J. Stephen Rhodes. Printed in the United States of America. All rights reserved. No part of this book may be reproduced in any manner except for brief quotations embodied in critical articles or reviews. For information address Wind Publications, 600 Overbrook Drive, Nicholasville, KY 40356

First edition

International Standard Book Number 978-1-893239-87-6
Library of Congress Control Number 2008934935

Front cover — Alexandra Rozenman's watercolor, "Rehearsal."
www.alexandrarozenman.com

I thank the Hambidge Center for Creative Arts and Sciences for their grant and much-needed space to bring this collection toward completion. For encouragement and for providing critique, I am grateful to Leatha Kendrick, Nancy Tupper Ling, Teresa Cader, Fred Marchant, Susanna Lang, Charlie Hughes, Andrea O'Brien, C.E. Morgan, and my friends from Frost Place and Stonecoast, particularly Baron Wormser, Jeffrey Harrison, Jeanne Marie Beaumont, Suzanne Cleary, and Dennis Nurkse. Last and most important, I am grateful for the editorial suggestions, patience, and support of my wife, Ann.

Acknowledgments
(Published or Forthcoming)

After Shocks, (Santa Lucia Books) Tom Lombardo, editor: "This New Never"
Comstock Review: "Answering Machine"
Connecticut Review: "Spring Fever"
Entelechy International: "Phingsten im Salzburg," "Heaven," "Night Bathing"
Freshwater: "I Want a Flag"
Goodfoot: "Boys, Unsupervised"
Heartland Review: "Swing Away;" "Still Life with Cup of Tea," "Candle"
International Poetry Review: "First Flower," "L,P,S–H"
Journal of the American Medical Association: "Interstate 75, Southbound"
Karamu: "Jungle Rot"
Kennesaw Review: "Mangoes," "This New Never"
Kudzu: "What You Heard"
Louisville Review: "Penitential"
Mad Poets Review: "In Flight"
Now and Then: "Ruah" (Published as "Western Wind")
Plainsongs: "Questions He Has"
Poetry Midwest: "Of Pond Scum and Other Damp Places"
Poetry Motel: "You"
Potomac Review: "Losing the Way"
Red Rock Review: "Sleeping with Julia"
Rock and Sling: "Things Passing"
Salamander: "On an Undeveloped Pasture"
Schuykill Valley Journal of the Arts: "Salome"
Shenandoah: "French Bread"
Sow's Ear Poetry Review: "My Imaginary Mother's Hat," "Demons in Seven Mile Canyon"
Tar River Poetry: "What Was Taken"
The Texas Review: "Morning Worship" (published as "Dead Again")
Timber Creek Review: "Jake's Gap on a Windy Night"
Willard and Maple, Pegasus (KY): "Music in Decline"
William and Mary Review, Comstock Review: "Cosmology"
Wind: "Colonoscopy"
Windhover: "Tales of the Idle Rich"

For my daughter, Rebecca Marie Rhodes, 1984-2005,

in memory.

"Neither death, nor life, nor anything . . . "
Romans 8:38-39

Contents

Introduction   1

I.

Morning Worship	5
Old Faithful	6
Demons in Seven Mile Canyon	7
Ruah	9
Things Passing	10
Phingsten im Salzburg	11
Penitential	12
My Imaginary Mother's Hat	13
This New Never	15
Tired	16
First Flower	17
For Once, Look Me in the Eye	18
Swing Away	19
I Want a Flag	20
Vegetables	21

II.

Beulaville, NC – 1969	25
Life in Space	27
Love in Disneyworld	28
Sleeping with Julia	29
Music in Decline	30
What You Heard	31
L,P,S—H	33
Single White Male, Fourteen	34
Heaven	36

Feeding the Crowd	37
Tree	38
Tales of the Idle Rich	39
Goodnight, Irene	40
Answering Machine	41
Spring Fever	43
Mangoes	44

III.

Cosmology	47
Losing the Way	48
Leaning on a Harley 883	57
French Bread	53
You	55
Questions He Has	56
Still Life with Cup of Tea, Candle	57
In Flight	59
Jungle Rot	61
Interstate 75, Southbound	62
Overburden	63
What Was Taken	64
Salome	65
Night Bathing	66
Of Pond Scum and Other Damp Places	67
Boys, Unsupervised	68
Saddle Mountain	59
Jake's Gap on a Windy Night	70
On an Undeveloped Pasture	71
Juniper, Mostly Dead	72
Colonoscopy	73
Stranger	74

Introduction

In his lovely, painful debut, Steve Rhodes has given us a book filled with grace. These poems do not profess the easy belief that passes for faith. They possess a distinctive voice that trusts the grace of an awkward and impassioned questioning. Spiritual seeker, part believer, part doubter, grieving father, lusty adolescent, emotionally defenseless son, lover of the material world, dancer who implores us to "Repent. Enjoy," Steve Rhodes seeks the divine everywhere — in "the aching skin of earth, filled again with a billion emerald nerves," in "the tan impossibilities of camouflaged uniforms," in "pond scum and other damp places," in the "windless silence" of desert places, and hardest of all, in "this new never" where he cannot call his daughter "to talk about [her] college course, on silence."

"Repent. Enjoy." These are the two poles of a collection that seeks the divine everywhere. The poems invoke desert saints and ex-wives, an imaginary mother and two views of a dinner with French bread. They dance in Heaven with all manner of celebrants, including Aunt Maxine, who "is sure I'm doomed, together with the Taliban." They sing in sonnets and in the musicality of free verse lines, in forms received and created, with an impish playfulness and in parables that make his spiritual journey palpable. It is a tribute to the range and craft of the book that the superb set of poems grieving his daughter's suicide do not overshadow the whole, but rather take their place as part of the fabric of a life spent asking hard questions.

The Time I Didn't Know What to Do Next is among the best new books I have read. Read it. Keep it close at hand. I'm betting you will continue to enjoy these poems and come to treasure this poet who has learned to "pick [his] own pockets for the sweet bread [he does] not know is there."

— Leatha Kendrick

I

Morning Worship

I woke up dead this morning,
listened for the sound of my heart,
instead heard the woodpecker
chunking pine, stripping
bark, like a torn old shirt.

I woke up dead, eyed
the curved edge of mountains
against the gray beyond
my window, the planet
driving from its center,
straining to break free.

Water in the creek, I awoke
dead. On oak leaves, water
in the pot on the stove.
I made water. Leaned into the sink
trembled, goose bumps, baptized.

Dead, I awoke again,
to the musty smell in the old house,
of pollen from the mullein in the yard
wafting new among dank walls.
Emparticled life.

Listen. Every day I wake up
dead all over again
at a loss for prayers.
Then the world says:
Water. Woodpecker.
Pollen. Earth.

Old Faithful

Earth rises, presses skyward, balloon
of lava beneath. Slow bloom of magma
strains earth cervix, millenniums of fire.
Fumaroles pant. Creation chants.

I want to carry a sign: *The time is coming.*
Deep throws steamwater jets, fresh stink
from silica volcanoes. Blue and yellow pools,
the hissing world sings. *Repent. Enjoy.*

One year a dog leaped into Celestine Pool.
Her master stripped off his shirt, jumped
into death. Too many smells of birth canals,
doorways to Precambrian, everything
compressed to a single point.

The chance to go down. Turn back, forswear
foolish ways, three blasts on earth's horn.
The whole park is going to blow, the ranger says.
Sulphur. Steam. Rivers of earth.
Who wouldn't jump? Who would?

Demons in Seven Mile Canyon

They love this windless silence
where kangaroo rats
and other scatabouts
forage like thieves
opening a safe at night.
They nudge each other
when I'm alone at my campsite
with the blanket to my neck.

When I start to go under,
they start to fly over
dropping bombs and propaganda:

You will be hungry tomorrow;
sharp teeth await you;
long-eared owls will eat your eyes;
no one will help.

Surely you heard them, Anthony,
patron of all who crave desolation.
You must have heard them cackling,
rubbing rough hands together
while you waited for sleep.

Did they stand by the door
to your dreams of seraphim,
then slam it shut
and trot out howling dogs?

No coyotes here,
except the ones in my head
who dared me to come alone
and fight among the junipers.

I came to face demons
in the wastes
where they wait,
licking their chops
for the Feast of All Souls.

Lead me to the table,
Holy Father of the Desert.
Guide me to my place
among them. Teach me
to laugh like a coyote,
to pick my own pockets
for the sweet bread
I do not know is there.

Ruah *

Clouds pour over ironweed and hickories—
swaddle in from Sioux Falls, St. Louis,
Paducah, Louisville, upside down cloths
from the west—headed next for Morgantown,
New York, or D.C. Slash pines bend, catkins fly
like a young girl's hair, undone.

You are there, inhabiting everything,
breath written not just on limbs
full of leaves but wound in each geode,
layered sandstone. You spin sub-atomic particles
in mysterious circles, turning unseen, West
to East. My own chest: Out. In.

Each day, whatever blows from Missouri,
you say something like, "Here, this place,
beloved. Wet your finger."

* (Hebrew) Breath, wind, spirit.

Things Passing

My grandfather jingled change in his pockets
when we strolled around the block. *Here*, he'd say,
*is where a Greek family lives, and here
is Ann White's kumquat.*

I sprang from the other side of the family. Men
whose eyes see six months ahead, the watchful,
who take the dog of their sadness for daily walks.

Sometimes faith means listening to wind.
When I was nine, my grandfather asked
What was that? Did you let a little poot?

Pfingsten Im Salzburg *

In pews flush with the faithful, fresh-scrubbed faces
wear reverence like short-collared jackets
worn by the men, rows of buttons down each lapel.
The organ swells the vaulted roof.
Priest follows cross, candles, and incense
to calm a thousand bees. To these, the white-robed youth

reads tongues of fire above each head,
a sound like wind, disciples seeming drunk, Medes,
Greeks, Persians, and Cappadocians hearing strange words
in their tongues and wondering at this noise—where
it comes from, why, for whom, for what.

Polite, the people in the pews sit safe,
hoping that by staying calm, perhaps
the fire will pass them by, simply smoke
to be inhaled a bit each May or June,
this yearly brush with a birth no more painful
than being split open with a fiery knife.

* Pentecost in Salzburg

Penitential

— For Marla Ruzicka

Out of the tan impossibilities of camouflaged uniforms
and antennaed vehicles, you draw the hand
of the brown-eyed girl and pull her on your lap
for photographers to see on our behalf, we who have lost
the ability to pray, *Deliver us from blood-guiltiness.*

Her hands rest on your knees, palpable in the way
her parents can no longer be, except in some hoped-for
paradise, ever-expanding from the red well in Mosul.
You skip the arguments and smile, politely begging
officers and diplomats for beds and new homes,
grinning your California grin, blond hair brushed back.

Whatever heaven you occupy, bring the wounded daily
to our doors, fasten their names to our gateposts,
wrap their pictures in leather on our forearms.
Purge us with hyssop. Grant children songs.

My Imaginary Mother's Hat

> There go my dark girls...
> Oh, they are lighter than flying dogs
> or the breath of dolphins.
> — *Anne Sexton*

I am afloat in a storm of farewells.
It is like the planet is drifting away from me
and I can't see even the stars.
The what-nextness of life is all I'm left with—
that and my imaginary mother's hat
that she used to hold to her head with her hand
while she grinned in the bow
of my imaginary father's speedboat.
Like the one Teddy Roosevelt
wore on San Juan Hill,
it is made out of green felt
with a brim that bends up in front

On the planet are cathedrals, office buildings
and six-lane highways, the Library of Congress
and the leaning tower of Pisa. Pope Julius
and Douglas MacArthur wave, as do
Mary Daly and Gloria Steinem. On the planet,
too, are the angels and archangels: Mom, Dad
my English teacher, Mr. Burrows,
Harry and Lester, who spoke grand words,
and others like J.J., Dixie,
and Anabelle, who taught me how to kiss.
They all grow smaller.

My imaginary mother loved fast boats
and horses. She was a jockey before
it was legal. She smoked cigars.
We hiked the Andes together.
She sends me postcards
with short messages:
Keep your head down. Start dancing
on your left foot first. You have the knack.
She is only there when I need her
really badly, like now.
She warned me over and over to be ready
to leave her and the world behind.

All I know is to put the hat on.
The instant I do, I know
my foot — my left foot —
will land on something hard. I will lean
into the gale and start to walk.
They say God is a wind.
I can believe it. I'm blowing away
from the earth, or it from me.
I have no idea where I am headed,
whether my imaginary mother will be there,
and whether she will be wearing her hat.

This New Never

This new never is quiet enough to fill a hundred caves
with monks. The wind rushes up from our pasture,
bends the pines and brings no news. I whisper
your name and look at your picture on the desk,
the one where you smile like the Little Flower
of Lisieux, willing your pain into someone else's joy,
if only you could decode the mysterious *how*.

You've been gone two months in this new forever
where I can't call you Sunday afternoons
to talk about your last college course, on silence,
a subject we both longed to comprehend and
entered in awkward minutes when we didn't know
what to say from the desert inside, each of us
craving the sound of wind across the mouths of caves.

Some days I swear not to eat. Then you make me break
my vow. You say, in my head, don't be stupid, and I want
to retort, *the way you were*, but don't because you hurt
enough, your eyes tired of looking for I'll-never-know-
what but perhaps a visit with one of your obscure poets
who helped you think yourself to that beach in Mexico
where you sat alone with the black dog watching the surf.

I look for any *ever* or *always* where you might be hiding,
your little girl self leaning out from behind the black oak
in our front yard, you in your pink and yellow dress
playing peekaboo with me. I listen to the sky. In the quiet
you speak: I'm not there, buddy. No dice. But I'm OK.

Tired

She pulled scared children to her. She went to trouble, loved
nursing homes. Spanish grabbed her, and the plays of Beckett.

Loretta Lynn and George Jones. Cheesy. She liked Faulkner.
Most weekends she wrote and read in her room with her stuffed dog.

Her friends stood in little groups after the funeral, lighting cigarettes
for each other, shuffling their feet in the snow, like orphans

waiting for their social worker, one like she planned to be—
Jane Addams crossed with Eugene Ionesco—art, justice, and love.

Cats jumped in her lap. She liked to walk the neighbor's dog after school.
She did not like to ask for help. Sometimes she cut herself

on the inside of her arms. She went to trouble. She grew tired
of getting it all right. She loved fuzzy things. Maybe she wanted a nap.

First Flower

God of the indefinite
walk between February
and March, show me
at least one bloodroot,
lone constellation
of white petals like
a preacher in her pulpit,
green single leaf,

or reveal a first anemone,
purple beside
a dormant poplar tree
whose buds wait
for the similar mercy
of opening to sky.

Mysterious, moving
woodland God,
stand still
long enough for me
to smell copper
galax she loved well,
like all things acid-sweet.

If you will not unveil
her, reveal nodding
trillium, Solomon's seal,
along this trail
of winter duff,
of still-brown leaves.

For Once, Look Me in the Eye

Bed made, dishes put away, prayers said,
at my desk to try again, looking out.
Snowflakes twist in eddies of wind,
turn scrub pines into restless hands.
The only stable feature is Saddle Mountain
gray and prone. My heart does its work,
ticks in tandem with the click
of wind-up clock I keep nearby but hate.
Your brother's arm upon your shoulder,
your sister's silver chain around your neck.
For once you look me in the eye, lean in
and smile from the leaded glass frame.
The beat in my chest, clock, breathing out, in.

Swing Away

Somewhere among the arcs on the swingset
I lost a bit of her, blond hair flying
out behind, banner to her mad delight
in her favorite childhood sport. She'd fling
her neck back, the way she did when I tried
to hold her close, as if to say she ran
on her own clock like the rest of us, I
suppose, only her resolve seemed planned
from before the first time she bowed away
while lying newborn on my chest. Maybe
she was warning us she would not stay
long but was bound for a new place
she could see when the ache inside made her
stretch to look around some last dark corner.

I Want a Flag

I'm not coming here any more
to this circle of grass surrounded
by asphalt, eight stones with names and dates
pressed flat against this green disc
with its Orthodox cross, tilted vases, and flag
sprouting from the words *World War Veteran*.

You were a veteran, too—of Paxil and Elavil,
and of a counselor who looked like Freud
biting his pencil at the funeral home while he said,
I don't know why she stopped showing up.
Your arms bore scars and stripes, some of them fresh.
You had a soldier's eyes, honey,
a soldier back from some extended tour,
your glance here for a minute, then gone.

Am I the widow, wife, mother? I'm sorry—father,
husband seem too tough for the way I feel.
I want a black dress, to ululate, to faint,
to have my friends carry me off while the mullah
rocks back and forth uttering. I want a flag.
I want it folded, brought to me,
to lay it on the stone, to trace the letters
that say your name but can never speak—
not in this bizarre country of crosses, stones,
and grass, this strange green disc.

Vegetables

One summer she sold vegetables at the co-op:
        tomatoes and carrots,
          jicama, loofah, and mache.
She wore a blue apron and put her hair under a red bandana,
            stood there with a paper bag while the man
                from Clarke Street fussed over the shiitake,
            squeezed each one.
She smiled when the lady who bought two pounds of parsnips
        each week told her
           she had pretty blue eyes.
That is what my daughter did that summer,

I guess. What she told me was her bosses were a pain
        but that she loved the vegetables and a few customers,
           like the lady who bought parsnips.

I crave vegetables now. Especially winter squash.
And turnips. I miss her eyes.

We had a deal when she came home: no meat.
Carrots, Dad. Buy me carrots and I'll be fine.

I planted pumpkins this year, weird ones with names
        like Jarrahdale and Winter Luxury Pie, some with bumps
           like acne, some that ripened gray.
I will plant more next summer, maybe parsnips and kale.

Blue eyes.

II

Beulaville, NC – 1969

— For Suzanne Cleary

The time I didn't know what to do next
I arranged my furniture in the little frame house

that sagged in the middle like an ark—
just three pieces really: a mattress, chair,

and desk made from a filing cabinet,
an old door, and some concrete blocks.

One stoplight town, diploma in hand, my bosses
instructed me to start the revolution, empower

the poor. I possessed no more than numbers
and facts, such as the pregnancy rate

for teenagers and median age, high, income,
low, for the place I now called home.

I knew no one. The neighbor who topped
and suckered tobacco for a dollar an hour

or his wife who made bologna bacon, bologna pie
and stew from surplus food, laughed in her kitchen,

*This surplus cheese is good. Take some
peanut butter and mix the two together.*

Her can-do cooking blew my must-do master
plans out the window—newspaper stories,

five year schemes, and charts and graphs,
the kind that lined our family business walls.

I called my father to say how helpless I felt,
he clicked his tongue, the sound of one hand clapping.

In the telephone booth, it was just the hiss of the line,
an encouraging "Goodbye," then the sound of wind

across tobacco fields and nearer,
blowing through bean vines. I didn't know

what to do next, so I did next to nothing
except sit in the kitchen and listen.

Life in Space

So, when did the props fall away like those hoses
and arms that drop off rockets as they start to rise?

You thought you would die when your dad flew off to Miami
again, and again, leaving you on a tether

your father called being a man. Kid,
I don't envy you those times, nor when your brother

boarded a plane for college a year early because
that's what smart boys did. That year, you started

a new school yourself, and Herbie and Wayne
were no longer the other two Musketeers

but aliens you used to know, sort of, you know?
Make new friends, your mother said right before

she fell down on the dining room floor
that night, framed by the light from the street lamp.

You wanted to fly when you heard your father say,
If she goes, I go, kid—you're on your own.

You didn't let your mind go there. You pondered space suits.
You thought about gravity—how it no longer applied.

Love in Disneyworld

I was a prince. The kind with gold epaulets and an eight-pointed star. *Your Excellency, may I present Roxie Millsap from Coral Reef Estates.* All the rides rushed toward walls of death, then whirled away from meteorites and pirates' swords. Roxie clung to my arm and screamed. On the street imaginary chrome wheels spun on my imaginary blue Malibu. My imaginary girlfriend brushed my cheek with her lips as she hopped out. *I like a man in a uniform*, she said. *I like a man with a souped-up car.*

Sleeping with Julia

Aside from your mouth, long legs,
and eyes that play, I want to sleep
with you one night to know what
you think in the limousine,
at the coffee machine,
or when you pray. Come on,
all of us do, it's a question
of where we send them wafting to.

I'd talk all night, even if it means
running around the bed,
to know what makes you cry,
not alligator tears, but the time
your father said nothing, but meant
O God, how I hurt, or when your mother
glared and you stared back.

I know something about that, about the time
the ambulance took my mother away,
about my father's dead eyes.
I want to lie on my side
next to you in my raggy boxer shorts—
you wear what you want.

Music In Decline

My mother's slip into silence was made fast
the day she bore gardenias to the rail
and wed my father's path, a trail
of graphs and numbers. Dispossessed
of teenaged minuets and concert halls,
her body conspired to make children
instead—her spirit more and more hidden.
My brother and I grew up within walls
my mother tended with angry ears. Because
she lost chords and melody,
so much turned flat for our family.
Beethoven and Brahms shrank to what was,
or worse, a one-note hum and numb no-sound.
She could not bear to have them around.

What You Heard

They told you to wait
for what you want:
cedary hair leaning close,
or your life. Don't

expect to see purple
at the rim of sky,
or an arm draped
around your neck,
or to rest,
not because you won't
sleep, but don't

hope for something
like peace and maybe
you will find it now
and then, the way
you do when picking
strawberries and you
find one so sweet
it tastes the way
you should far more
often. Don't

believe in a sun
you cannot see
even though fog
looks full of light.
Believe in the slap

of wave on rocks,
jostle of crowd,
pull and unhappy
push. Think
of yourself perhaps
as a hawk
or sandhill crane,
high and singing,
smelling the wind,
hoping, but don't.

L, P, S – H

I turn on the faucet. Hundreds of letters fly out like bats. Noteworthy are *L* and *P*. Let's play, lover. Please leave, Pete. Also, *S* — sucker, succor, suck her, suture, suit yourself. When the sink is packed, I cut the water back, sit and stare at the universe of discourse. Sly lust plies its showy legs. Prayers lift skyward. Politicians let sense lull in laws. I plunge my hand in, pull out a line: *Sorrow purges love of its shine*. I hang it out to dry outside with others: *Learn to live with pain*, and the only one with an *H* — *Help!*

Single, White Male, Fourteen

He gives
up on dancing
for the night and starts
to smoke with all the guys who hang
out in

the men's
room. They hold their
cigarettes up to the vent
on the hand dryer and watch them spark,
mini-

fireworks
displays. They stand
there together, egging
each other on, something about
Freddy's

car and
Annie Woolsey,
who he longs to slow-dance
with some day. In his dream they play
Theme From

a Summer Place,
while she runs her
arms around his shoulders,
breathes on his neck, and in the dream
she sees

he's not
a hyena
like the rest of the gang,
even though he suspects they're not,
either

while they
laugh at the same
jokes over and over
again, this night involving
body

parts, large
fruit, and things like
zucchini squash. He's still
laughing with the pack at
midnight

when they
turn out the lights,
and everyone goes home,
even Annie, and he ends
up in

his room
again, and it's
no different really, from
the men's room because it's safe,
sort of.

Heaven

Last night I dreamed I saw girls
in gray hijabs spinning with Hassidim,
monks with bowls in hands, a priestess
with an upraised cup. I was in the circle
with Aunt Maxine from Perryville,
whose son was killed last year in Kandahar,
who thinks I am too soft on sin,
the evil *them* and all unholy things.

Maxine is sure I'm doomed, together
with the Taliban and certain people
on her street, but in my dream
she twirled with me, girls with hidden faces,
monks and nuns, men with curls and hats,
her head thrown back, to take in
Cygnus, Mars, the Pleiades.

Feeding the Crowd

In the middle of *I want to be*
        remains *I am*. The stubborn
        otherness I resist contains
over and over again, *I was*:
        the time I shut the door
        on my daughter's fingers,
the broken vase my wife adored,
        when I said brassiere meaning bizarre,
        or when I said I didn't care
any more. I did. Just too tight
        to let softness pour out
        like water from a jar.

Maybe beneath *I was*
        is *I really am*, somewhere,
        the boy who brought loaves
and fishes to Christ, sometime
        in my *might have been*,
        the one who started passing
baskets around to the hungry crowd,
        baskets that came back fuller
        than they were, somehow,
full of laughter, overlooked mistakes
        and sins, forgotten *should have beens* —
        flowing over with *will be*.

Tree

It was the one that loomed
over the driveway, brooded
every time I drove by,
one side sleek, bark like
pantyhose pulled tight,
as if the tree were saying,
Hi there good-looking,
the other side sprung open,
unbuckled like a corset
undone on a spinster
laid out at a funeral home.

It leaned at the gravel drive
the way girls did at cotillions
when they smoked cigarettes
and looked out at the lake
and moon, talking softly;
the way, before she died,
the old woman stopped
rocking and craned her neck
from her porch when I started
up the hill, home again from work.

Hung out over the driveway
like a pole full of prayer flags,
burden of longing, the place
in the surrounding canopy
where it fell now space
in the dusk for coquettish sun
among the blackberries
and hobblebush, I miss
its nosiness, its desire.

Tales of the Idle Rich

The idle rich watch the news and roll their fingers
on armchairs like a wave on a pond. Some nap
before supper. They brush their teeth, get headaches
once or twice a week. Many need extra fiber.

The idle rich like and dislike their cousins
from Cincinnati and Omaha. They can play
Clementi's *First Sonatina*—or not.
The idle rich can be bigoted and fair on the same day.
They like baseball, at least in principle, in September.

The idle rich walk softly from the bed,
when they cannot sleep, just as you do because
your husband wakes at the drop of a hat.
On occasion, when alone, the idle rich
watch late night television. They drink warm milk.

The idle rich listen to the sounds of crickets at night
and wonder what it is like to pray to the God
of all mercies not to be fired. They pray
like you: *Please let me be necessary.*

Goodnight, Irene

Light from the single bulb at the top of the stairs cut
across my waist—my legs twitching under the quilt in the dark,

my head in the yellow straight-edged strip that divided
false day from night. I waited for the creak from the bottom

of the stairs, my mother come to say goodnight.
I lay there waiting, Raggedy Andy in shadow, Hardy Boys

in the dusk. She pressed down on the bed and began to rub
my shoulders, talking me down the way one would

a skittish horse. What, I asked, would happen to me
if you were no longer there, you know, not here any more.

She smiled: There will always be someone. I pictured
my uncle, holding a cigarette, looking annoyed,

and my grandfather who rarely broke a grin, and I prayed.
And there's always God, she said, but I'm not going

anywhere, not any time soon at any rate, and then sang
for me, Goodnight, Irene. Irene, Goodnight.

Answering Machine

On the off chance
you were home
I declined to call,
afraid to hear your
hello, the way you kept
the chain on your voice,
waiting for assurance your
caller was not a creep or
shill for the state police
or Viet Nam vets.
On the answering machine
God was in the midst of you,
who would not be moved.

This you I loved to leave
a message for: I have gone
to a far country, dear,
I have taken my father's
inheritance—this truth
I hold to be self-evident
no matter how I stutter
before your wary ears.

The taped and bolder you
made a bolder me. Ten seconds
of your voice gave me
time to dissemble,
design a firm retort,
play on your words,

pretend a self behind
the automatic switch
that turned the unreal you
from off to on.

Spring Fever

Dogs loll at my feet while a cardinal mimics
Caruso, a chorus of lawnmowers behind him
singing the end of winter chanson. I am drunk
with the afternoon slant of the sun that puts its hand
down my chest saying, *Hi there big boy, want to play?*

Sleepy and in heat at the same time, I want to go
barefoot on Tahiti with Gauguin, disporting myself
with the women, bee among guava blooms.

I am a godly man who says with the people,
The temple of the Lord, the temple of the Lord,
as if that brings clear-sightedness in late April,
the time when all you can see is the aching skin
of earth filled again with a billion emerald nerves
saying, *Touch me,* the prayer of the cosmos—O,

I want to roll in pastures like a dog,
legs in the air, spine writhing back and forth, spreading
life like pollen, and you are in—kiss me in your mind—
Ohio, across the muddy river where it is still gray
and spring, a thing undone.

Mangoes

The telephone rings. I make the same mistake
again and answer. My worry pushes
my hand to the phone when all I want to do
is sell mangoes in Corazon. You
want to talk about your sad marriage.
I want to be nice. The mangoes
glow in the sun. Across from my stand
are blue and yellow hammocks and the woman
who pours red soda into plastic bags
and punches them with straws. You say you dread
your wife the way I fear the sound of cars in the rain.
You cannot leave, you say, it would be wrong.
I would flee tonight. I would pass through clouds,
eat mangoes, lean back against the palm.

Cosmology

Underneath Orion hang Jupiter, the Perseids,
and our moon that I cannot see right now
for all the stratocumulus—I think—clouds.

Beneath clouds, rain; beneath rain, the gabled roof,
low in front and high in back because of
the slope of the red clay hill our house sits on.

Below the roof, our bedroom and the bed
on which we sat this morning like marionettes
whose strings are loose but not necessarily undone,

you and I like strangers again, the way we need
to be now and then to make friends with the odd guests
who spring up inside us, old ghosts we have lain aside,

or tried to. Below your skin, your beating heart
and memories of your father's tight grip on the handle
to your door, his need to be right, or better, have you wrong.

Beneath my skull, a brain adept at subterfuge
because what I want is for you not to be
my room-invading mother whose love was like a cloud—

large, hovering, and close, but not too easy
to touch, hiding lightning but just as often
dissipating into empty dark. Below us,

the floor we both stood on when we made up
and held each other with relief for the parents we were not
and for the ones we would not be. Underneath,

the years together: the dancing—pulling apart,
coming close, what ties us tight and holds us up.
Beneath our floor, the footings and basement,

clay, shale, slate and stone sunk deep in mystery,
like what bound us together and supported us
this morning, both what hovers and lies beneath.

Losing the Way

You know how we hiked in the woods—
the way we switched places, trading the lead
when we walked off-trail, so one of our brains
could rest, so one set of eyes could see
clear paths through rhododendron?
You remember the laurel hell, going on
hands and knees, the blackberry bogs?
How, down by Buck Fork, we fixed tea
on a sandstone boulder standing in the creek
while the rain stopped for a few minutes?
How we sang, *You get wrinkles on your face;
pruney gets them every place*, and the dirty song
about Elrod Scoggins, our imaginary hiking friend?

So, as they say, was it something I said—
some awkward turn in theology,
or too much of it, that stopped our yearly trips?
Was it you—some quiet shutting down
or turning off; your wife, your work,
a swing in your state of mind?
Did I strut too much after they hung the blue hood
around my neck while Desmond Tutu watched?
Your stopped returning my calls.
I stopped calling you back.

Up Kephart Spur, past Laurel Gap, I still hike
to Sterling every other year and chase in my mind
the by-all-that-is-holy bear from our food
with the flaming branch in my hand, you calling me
Moses and a lot of other things while the other campers

looked on as if we were one part mountain men—
Daniel Boones—and two parts fools, come to disturb
their sleep the way you do, occasionally still, my own—
you looking back, warning me to step left
of the sandstone boulder in the creek, not right,
saying it's time to trade places again, that you need
to rest your mind, the way now I need to rest mine.

Leaning on a Harley 883

Isn't there an easier way
than this to be kissed
on the eyelids, she asked
the flat-eyed boy with chain tattoos
on his arms, to which he said,
let's go for a ride
and flicked his cigarette aside.
There isn't, he said.

She told him she prayed
to St. Agnes at night
for pure thoughts but also
earthly joy. He said,
I used to pray to be
my momma's only boy,

which came true at the time,
when my dad fled to Maine,
never to return. She said,
I wonder if he's out there —
God. I'd like to know why
when you get it all right,
your mother will die
or the police will come,

and when you mess up,
now and then the sun pours
on your back, warm hands
from the sky; or your brother
comes home from the war alive.
I have no idea, he replied,

sometimes I'd rather be dead,
or maybe I'd live in a house
in the woods that would look
like the sun about to rise.
Then she asked, couldn't it look
like it's going to set, as well,

to which he replied,
I do pray, you know;
I still ask God for a surprise
now and then.
You ask too many questions.
He kissed her eyelids,
pulled on his helmet,
and tightened the strap
beneath his chin.

French Bread

The night I took your shoe off
under the table at *La Chanson*,
under the artichoke
and basket of bread, you smiled
and I knew we could do, as Paul says,
all things together good.
But throw it on the water now,
the French bread you buttered
and moaned about.
Just go.

Your foot under the table,
like the tip of a cat's tail,
belied your Mary Poppins smirk.
Somewhere between
your purse-lipped grin and shoe
I got lost. Go down, Moses,
let it go.

To watch you roll your eyes
while eating the baguette
was sacrament enough.
I kiss it goodbye in God's mercy,
the bread, the wine, your rising up
and sitting down, and the way
you said *stop,* often meaning
go.

Last night at another bistro,
your head flown to a different city,

your eyes glared past my shoulder
while you framed words like,
It never would have, and
You yourself have said. All the time
your shoes snug on your feet,
your hands nimbly buttered bread,
daughter of Jerusalem, your cheeks
comely with ornaments,
just go.

You

are like a Red-cockaded woodpecker
pretending to be endangered
at a conference on bio-diversity
while stuffing yourself on canapes
like wood beetles. You
cackle your woodpeckery
laugh while the scientist
beside you is ablaze with eyes
that follow your measured nods,
you in your black cocktail dress
with the flash of red that says,
You have not seen me here before.

You cut your eyes at me just once
to say, unspeaking, *Nice try,*
Buster, but I will fly on
to the next tree now. Goodbye.

Questions He Has

What about the way you straighten every book
on your shelves until they look like a poster
of famous doorways in Paris or of different kinds of peppers
in neat rows — yellow, red, and green — only your roster
lays out Steinem, Friedan, De Beauvoir, and Sand?

What about how you squeeze blood from the steering wheel
when you drive? *Move it or lose it*, you declaim,
shoulders curling tighter toward the dashboard,
fingers red or white, nothing in-between?

What about the way you debate the price of tea
in coffee shops, then demand to know
where the beans come from, *some place quasi-free*?

What about the soft words you used to say
in the back seat of his car, eyes wide?

What about how you used to let him have his way?

Still Life with Cup of Tea, Candle

I follow you up the mountain trail
    across the bridge below the pond
        by cattails bent against the rocky bank
            and hanker for a fire in the shack
                with one rectangle eye

You frown like a cat worried with its tail
    talk about loose ends
        but I said
        then he said
        no one seems to understand
            twirling untwirling
            your hair

I fix tea on the stove
    rose hips with peppermint
        you curl your legs on the faded chair
            look out the window at little waves
                steam wends from the cup
                    your eyes unwind

Do you keep coming back to learn
    how to listen
        to watch water riffle the gravel beach

You ask how I am

A single piece of driftwood
    floats up and down

    Later a candle
        I whisper about the rattle
            of cattails
                ripple of stream
                      you unravel your hand

In Flight

— For Maury

Into the booth we slide —
me quickly with ease,
you slow to bend your knees —
while your wife helps you glide,

her fingers soft wrenches
calibrated to give support
without the look of effort,
her mouth pouring sentences

about your church, the work
you used to do for the schools,
how she has to choose
your shoes now, your shirt —

you who sailed a football
sixty yards downfield
in a spiraled arc that sealed
the win for us that fall

when we two read eight books
in three days for history,
on Augustus, Cato, Pliny,
the Senate, Agrippina's hooks

in Tiberius's soul.
I ask for egg foo yung.
She orders chicken almond ding
her choice for you both.

With a glint you pointed
downfield and said run,
reminded us about the sun,
and when we scored, acquainted

me with a self I never thought
to find in my severe home.
You laughed at studying Rome
two nights before we got

the ancient history test.
Your wife picks up your spoon
to feed you again,
while your eyes are steadfast

on mine, unblinking,
holding to this last time
we will likely dine
together. This evening

I want to fly downfield
again under your throw,
run where you want me to go,
away from what is now revealed

Jungle Rot

— For Brian

He gave it up last night
after the firefight.
He began to doubt
the times in Georgia

when he smoked a cigarette
and watched waterbugs walk
like Jesus across deep pools
that shone in sun on the Etowah.

He gave up on trout rising to mayflies,
on the phoebe's dance out and back,
the rattle of the pine warbler,
and the water song of the river.

He turned into a slow moan,
the sound of Buddhist monks,
the widow in Chu Lai,
palm trees bending,

mud-covered boots,
and night wind at Da Nang,
bringing with it
the smell of rain.

Interstate 75, Southbound

In a snowy blur North of Knoxville,
a white cross spells *Jason* on its spar.

Near Athens on a rail, two ribboned hearts.
White letters spell *Sheila*; mud stains the *e* in *Sue*.

Winter culls, the elders say,
The weary head home.

Three gold crosses near Cartersville,
no names, plastic roses on a hill.

Overburden

Who let the sun shine here
where it never did, made rough places
smooth, high places low,
cleared a hole for the moon?

People don't say *world without end*
anymore, never speak about where
the sun don't shine, or we'll meet again,
don't know where don't know when

the mountains will ever dance,
their partners turned into plains.
Rows of vapor lights dominate
the night — hide nothing, hold nothing back.

What Was Taken

They stole the roto-tiller and mower
from the shed last night. Tonight it's hard to sleep
because the door still swings open in my mind
letting in strange fingers I might have seen
today putting coins in a parking meter
or shaking out cigarettes while I walked
by and waved the way I often do
to our townspeople—people with big hands,
rough-fingered and smooth, small hands, delicate
wrists. The sound of low voices and grunting,
maybe I hear them one night later
through the darkness in my mind and in the yard—
Neighbors on a quiet errand,
people I thought I knew but don't, reach
into my sleep, steal from me one thing more.

Salome

*— After the painting by
Lucas Cranach the Elder*

Her eyes rest just above your shoulder,
as you walk by and stop as if to talk
with a glass of wine in your hand. She is polite,
her face a bowl of self-assurance
laced with the comity of a princess.
Every fold of her sleeve, each gold link,
each necklace, perfect. Her bodice fits tight
on her breasts as do her lips on her mouth.
Elegantly smug, she needs no words.
How many of these, who, smiling,
asking for blood, must we endure?
How many silver platters,
bearing heads of saints.

Night Bathing

My hand brushes her arm, and my friend,
cousin to ghost crabs and terns,
shoves me back the way Skull Creek
turns each tide. Footsteps, she says.
What she hears are her father's feet
on the sand at her door, the grinding sound
of his shoes on a cigarette,
while she slowly takes off her dress
to steal down to the sea.

Of Pond Scum
and Other Damp Places

I'd lie to you if I didn't say
I love it when my shoes get wet
on the muddy banks of ponds.
My own sweat, the oil
behind my ears, the stored ripe smells
yank me to steamy islands
in the dark sea no one sees
beneath my skin. Since God made
all wet things, who am I
to turn up my nose at my outpourings
each morning? All of it—
part of some great watery plan.

Scum from pollen in backwaters,
kelp that undulates by rocky shores,
jetsam by ship docks—
I swirl them with my finger.
What is clammy damp is where birth comes.

Boys, Unsupervised

They eye the falls from the pool below,
like a school of salmon as they flex
and laugh loud, the way boy-men do
when confused, their knee-length shorts
sticking to their legs, ballooning
when they swim. They yell
at the bald and bold one with rings
in his ears who clambers up rocks and waits.

Thirty feet up, his friends say *stop*;
thirty feet down, they start a chant.
He finds his feet at the edge and throws
his weight into the space
between already and not yet.
He understands for three seconds
manhood, love, stars and hate,
then shatters what was smooth above,
sputters, and swims to rocks again,
the way boy-men do, when confused.

Saddle Mountain

Saddle Mountain draws
to the sky in the morning,
wearing a gray pause

before mottled green
climbs from the pinnacle's feet
and softens again

already thicker
branches awaiting new leaves
to sprout and flicker.

Soon, it will be hard
to see the trunks and branches—
tree skeletons—wired

together by roots
in the mountain's rocky skin.
Unceasing wind mutes

the ridgeline's passing,
almost past, simplicities
beneath clouds massing

like armies of change.
Later, all will be hidden.
Each limb will arrange

leaves, catkins, flowers,
and fruit to conceal what is
shown these final hours

of raw exposure,
of nude, silver-barked branches,
things appearing pure.

Jake's Gap on a Windy Night

Stars stay in the wooded cylinder above our fire,
while sparks spread above the leaves, lighting night,
burning themselves out. We glimpse
Orion's legs and the hint sent down
from Pegasus that more will be revealed.

Mountains gather us in and push stars away
from the gap where we sleep in our tent.
When we wake at four, Big Bear has chased Little
further north. Trees lean over us,
curious beasts whose noisy paws
blot out lights from other galaxies.

On an Undeveloped Pasture

— *After William Stafford*

This is a field where tractors do not disc,
where a supermarket does not stand.
This is a field where weeds are welcome
and given names like Blue Star grass and Kingdom Come,
and the only constant thing is land.

Deer walk here,
their tails like elf lanterns in the dusk.
No strip mall. What gives profit
rides wind: goldenrod, milkweed, dust.

Juniper, Mostly Dead

Its silhouette
on the sagebrush hill
makes it look
like Kokopelli,
or maybe Hunter,
except it tilts,
a little drunk,
as if it cannot
get the sacred dance
just right
and all it knows
to do is offer
one green bough
to wind-pushed sky.

Colonoscopy

This is not really
about the
half inch
tube
that
blazes
trails to
hinterlands
under the
gaze of masked
experts whose
probe
slithers
past prostate
bladder kidneys
like a reptilian
homing pigeon
searching for
malignant
roosts
within
the *cloaca*
maxima.

This is not about
the day before,
of purging
"cleansing"
dietary penance
begging for absolution

at a porcelain throne
nor is this about cramps
weak legs
willfully drinking
anatomical
poison
for some greater
good.

This is about
Teach us
to count our days
about seeing the sun
strike oaks
at dawn with
shades of
pink
that take
away the breath
about tasting
new sunlight.

Stranger

I have talks with myself in the morning.
Sometimes I kneel
or sing. I always read
words from saints, at least those I see

as such. Making my home in their minds
for a few moments,
I live with Crone's disease,
say, or on San Salvador's streets in the seventies.

I hear myself speak to power
as if I did not have it,
and let myself live
somewhere other than the here I'm given

perhaps by God, but even if not
I allow myself a bit
of courage, at least
in another's mind and distant place.

I dream of having enough faith
to live in my own skin
and face ghosts
who argue for cautious and stingy love at most.

God help me, some times I pray
for a new heart
or a changing one
to embrace the stranger inside I am called to become.

Printed in the United States
127670LV00003B/2/P